American Culture & Conflict

Living Through the Civil War

Yvette LaPierre

rourkeeducationalmedia.com

Before & After Reading Activities

Before Reading:

Building Academic Vocabulary and Background Knowledge

Before reading a book, it is important to tap into what your child or students already know about the topic. This will help them develop their vocabulary, increase their reading comprehension, and make connections across the curriculum.

1. Look at the cover of the book. What will this book be about?
2. What do you already know about the topic?
3. Let's study the Table of Contents. What will you learn about in the book's chapters?
4. What would you like to learn about this topic? Do you think you might learn about it from this book? Why or why not?
5. Use a reading journal to write about your knowledge of this topic. Record what you already know about the topic and what you hope to learn about the topic.
6. Read the book.
7. In your reading journal, record what you learned about the topic and your response to the book.
8. After reading the book complete the activities below.

Content Area Vocabulary

Read the list. What do these words mean?

abolish

amateurs

casualty

Confederate

currency

plantations

prohibit

sanitation

telegraph

Union

After Reading:

Comprehension and Extension Activity

After reading the book, work on the following questions with your child or students in order to check their level of reading comprehension and content mastery.

1. Why did the Civil War start? (Summarize)
2. Why was keeping slavery legal important to the southern states? (Infer)
3. How did women help the war effort? (Asking Questions)
4. What might your life have been like if you had lived during the Civil War? (Text to Self Connection)
5. What is an example of how the Civil War changed the United States? (Asking Questions)

Extension Activity

Pick one of the people mentioned in this book and do more research on him or her. What was the person's life like before the war? After the war? What new or surprising information did you learn?

Table of Contents

A Divided Nation 4
Slavery in America 10
Economy, Industry, and Innovations 16
Culture and Communication 22
Daily Life 26
Changing Roles of Women 34
Reuniting the Nation 40
Glossary 46
Index 47
Show What You Know 47
Further Reading 47
About the Author 48

Key Events

March 20, 1852:	Harriet Beecher Stowe's novel *Uncle Tom's Cabin* is published
November 6, 1860:	Abraham Lincoln elected as U.S. President
December 20, 1860:	South Carolina is first state to secede from the Union
July 21, 1861:	First major battle of the Civil War is fought
August 5, 1861:	Lincoln signs Revenue Act of 1861
1862:	Mary Jane Patterson, a former slave, becomes first African-American woman to earn a college degree
January 1, 1863:	Emancipation Proclamation signed by Lincoln
1863:	Mary Walker becomes first woman U.S. Army surgeon
April 9, 1865:	Gen. Robert E. Lee surrenders his Confederate army to Gen. Ulysses S. Grant
April 15, 1865:	Lincoln assassinated
August 20, 1866:	President Andrew Johnson issues a proclamation announcing the end of the Civil War

CHAPTER ONE

A Divided Nation

The first full battle of the American Civil War took place on a summer day in 1861. People rode buggies from Washington, D.C., to the battle site near Manassas, Virginia. Some packed picnic baskets. Men, women, and children came to cheer the **Union** troops to victory. The battle started. The smaller **Confederate** army forced the Union army to retreat. The picnickers were swept up in the panic. Clearly, the war would not end quickly as many had hoped.

The first full battle of the war on July 21, 1861, was called the First Battle of Bull Run by Union forces and the First Battle of Manassas by Confederate forces. There were thousands of casualties on both sides.

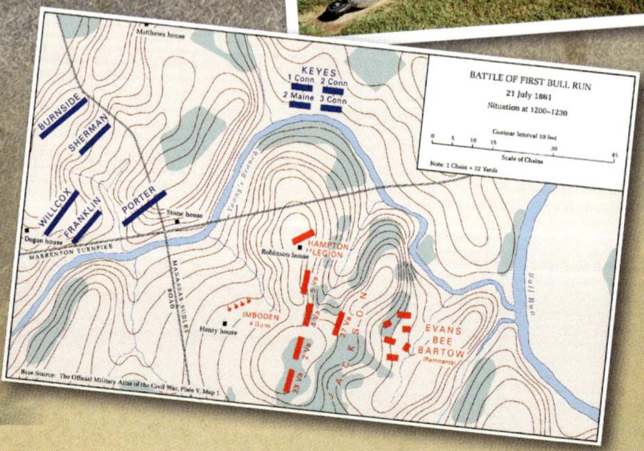

The Civil War started because of disagreements between northern and southern states in the Union. The most important disagreement involved slavery. Slavery was illegal in the North but still legal in the South.

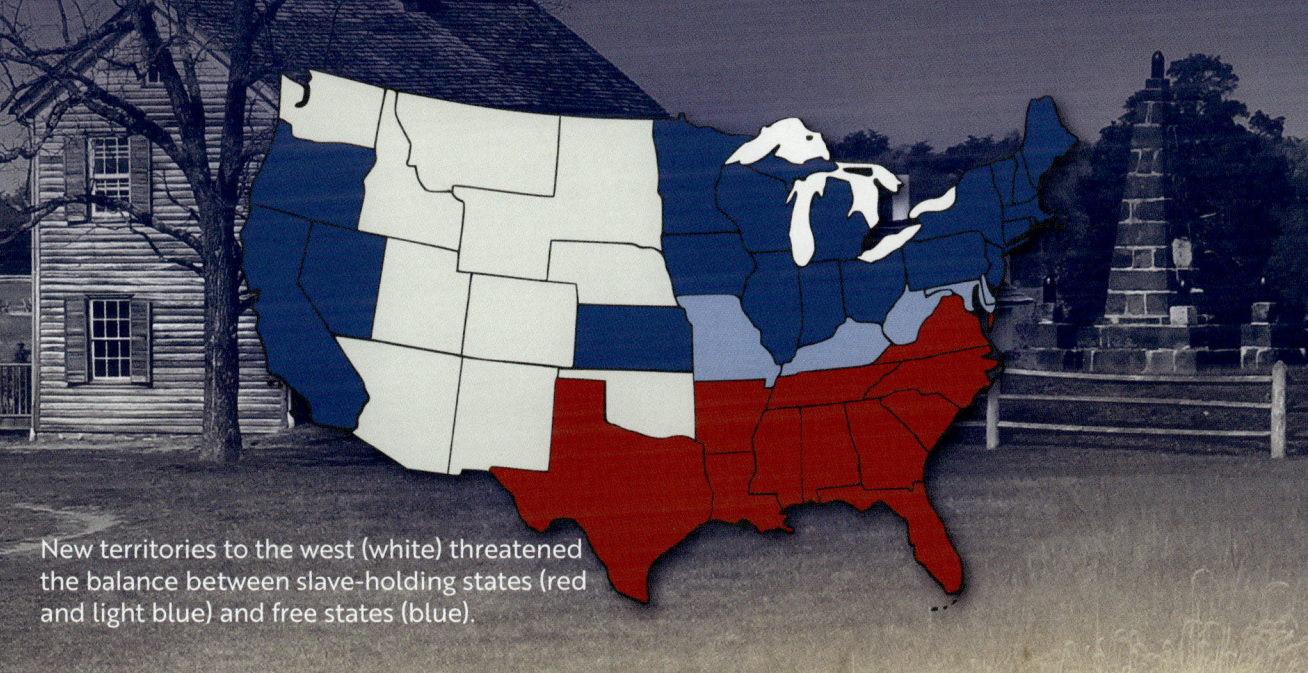

New territories to the west (white) threatened the balance between slave-holding states (red and light blue) and free states (blue).

Harriet Beecher Stowe published her novel Uncle Tom's Cabin *in 1852. It described the cruelty of slavery. The book sold 300,000 copies in its first year. It persuaded many readers that slavery was wrong, and the movement against slavery grew.*

The country was expanding to the west. Abraham Lincoln and the new Republican Party wanted to **prohibit** slavery in new states. Southerners wanted each new state to be able to decide for itself.

Abraham Lincoln was elected President of the United States in 1860. Slave-holding states feared slavery would become illegal everywhere. Several seceded, or left, the Union. They formed a new nation called the Confederate States of America.

President Abraham Lincoln
February 12, 1809 – April 15, 1865

South Carolina was the first state to secede in 1860, followed by six others. Several states between the North and the South were undecided. Slavery was legal in these states, but they hadn't joined the Confederacy. Lincoln promised to end slavery in the border states if they would stay in the Union.

The Union flag during the Civil War had 34 stars for the 34 states. The southern states were still represented on the flag because the Confederacy's declaration of secession was considered illegal by the federal government.

Eventually President Lincoln declared war against the Confederacy. He wanted to keep the states together. The war raised many important issues for Americans.

On April 12, 1861, Confederate troops opened fire on Union troops at Fort Sumter in South Carolina to start the Civil War. The bombardment lasted 34 hours. Finally, Union forces surrendered without any casualties.

Would the Union be preserved? What kind of government would the future bring? Would the war bring freedom to slaves? Citizens would have to live through four difficult years of war to know the answers to those questions.

Soldiers drawing water from a well

Civil War veteran with family

CHAPTER TWO

SLAVERY IN AMERICA

By 1867, more than 10 million African slaves were in the Americas.

The United States was the largest slave-holding country in the world by the time of the Civil War. Starting in the 1600s, slave traders captured men, women, and children in West Africa. They forced them onto ships. Once the Africans arrived in America, they were sold as slaves.

Slave families tried to stay together but often were separated by white owners.

Slaves were still bought and sold in the South during the Civil War.

Slave trade from Africa was banned by the Slave Trade Act in 1807. The ban became effective January 1, 1808. By then, as many as one million Africans already were enslaved in America. Their children automatically became slaves to be bought and sold.

Africans had lives rich in language and art in their homelands. In America, they were not allowed to read and write. Despite that, a slave named Phillis Wheatley wrote poetry in the 1700s. Born in Africa and enslaved as a young girl, Wheatley became the first published African-American poet.

Enslaved people were forced to work for their owners for no pay. Most worked on **plantations** in the South. They planted, tended, and harvested crops such as cotton and tobacco. They worked from sunrise until after dark in all kinds of weather. Children as young as five worked in the fields.

A wagon is loaded with bales of cotton.

Some slaves worked in their owners' houses. They served as maids, cooks, and butlers. They cared for their owners' children. Others worked as blacksmiths, carpenters, and other skilled laborers.

It's thought that more than 100,000 slaves escaped to the North using the Underground Railroad.

Some people wanted to abolish all slavery. They were called abolitionists. They helped slaves escape to freedom in the North. Runaway slaves traveled at night in darkness. They followed secret routes to safe houses. This network of "stations" and "conductors" became known as the Underground Railroad.

Most of the cabins in the time of slavery were built to contain two families; some had partitions, others had none.

Slaves had no rights and often lived in terrible conditions. Many lived in one-room cabins with dirt floors. They had few clothes and little food to eat.

They were punished by their owners. Even worse, owners could divide up families and sell members far away. Some risked whippings if they tried to escape. For slaves, the Civil War was all about freedom.

Runaway slaves who were caught were brutally punished.

Harriet Tubman
c. 1820 – March 10, 1913

Harriet Tubman was one of the most famous conductors on the Underground Railroad. She had escaped slavery herself. She returned to the South 19 times over ten years to help runaways. She guided more than 300 people to freedom. She risked her own freedom to help others.

Slaves were shackled to keep them from running away.

CHAPTER THREE

Economy, Industry, and Innovations

The Civil War had major effects on the economies of the North and South. Before the war began, the North had been investing in railroads and factories for years. City streets bustled with European immigrants attracted by the plentiful factory jobs.

Factories and railroads gave the North an advantage during the war.

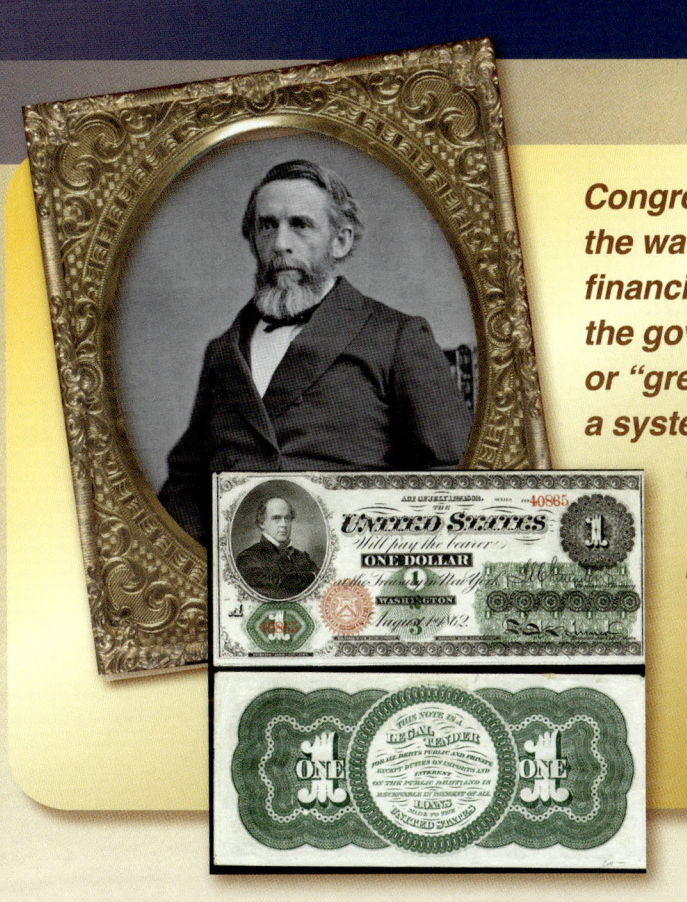

Congress passed several bills during the war that changed the American financial system forever. One allowed the government to print paper money, or "greenbacks." Another created a system of national banks and currency. The Revenue Act of 1861 established the first personal income tax to help pay for the war.

Top: George S. Boutwell (1818 – 1905), First Commissioner of Internal Revenue under President Lincoln
Bottom: Printed currency

Banks and shops lined the streets. On farms, machines helped with the planting and harvesting. The economy of the North grew throughout the war.

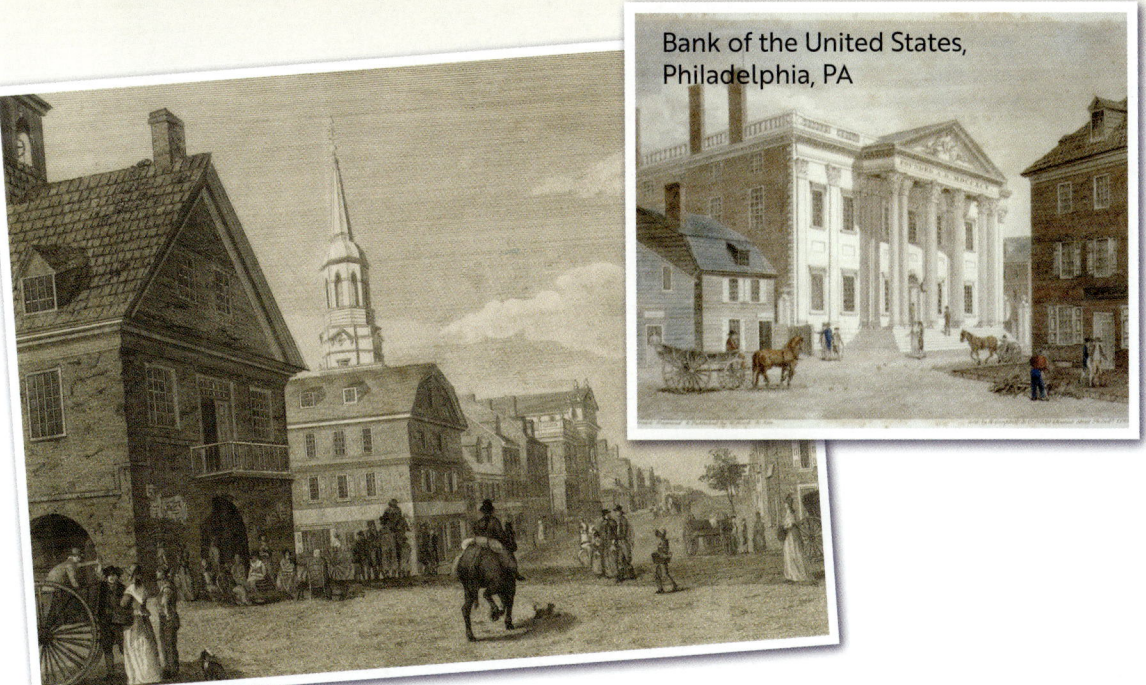

Bank of the United States, Philadelphia, PA

Agriculture was the biggest industry in the South. There were few factories. Wealthy farmers relied on slaves to work the fields. As the war progressed, fewer men and slaves were left to tend crops. The Union army blocked ports so that goods could not get in or out of the South. The economy grew worse, and many Southerners did not have enough food or clothes.

Slaves of all ages were forced to work long hours picking cotton in the fields.

The Civil War spurred advancements in several fields, including firearms and medicine. Rifles improved throughout the war. They became easier to load and more accurate. Early machine guns were invented during the war.

Above: A hot air balloon is raised
Right: A grounded hot air balloon

The Union army used hot air balloons during the Civil War to get a better view of the enemy. The balloon was tethered to the ground. A telegraph wire ran from the basket. From high in the air, the person in the basket could report on the location of Confederate soldiers.

Better weapons meant more wounded soldiers. Medicine advanced quickly as doctors and nurses treated thousands of soldiers. Early in the war, hospitals were disorganized and dirty. Many soldiers died from infections.

Fredericksburg, Virgina, hospital with wounded soldiers in 1864

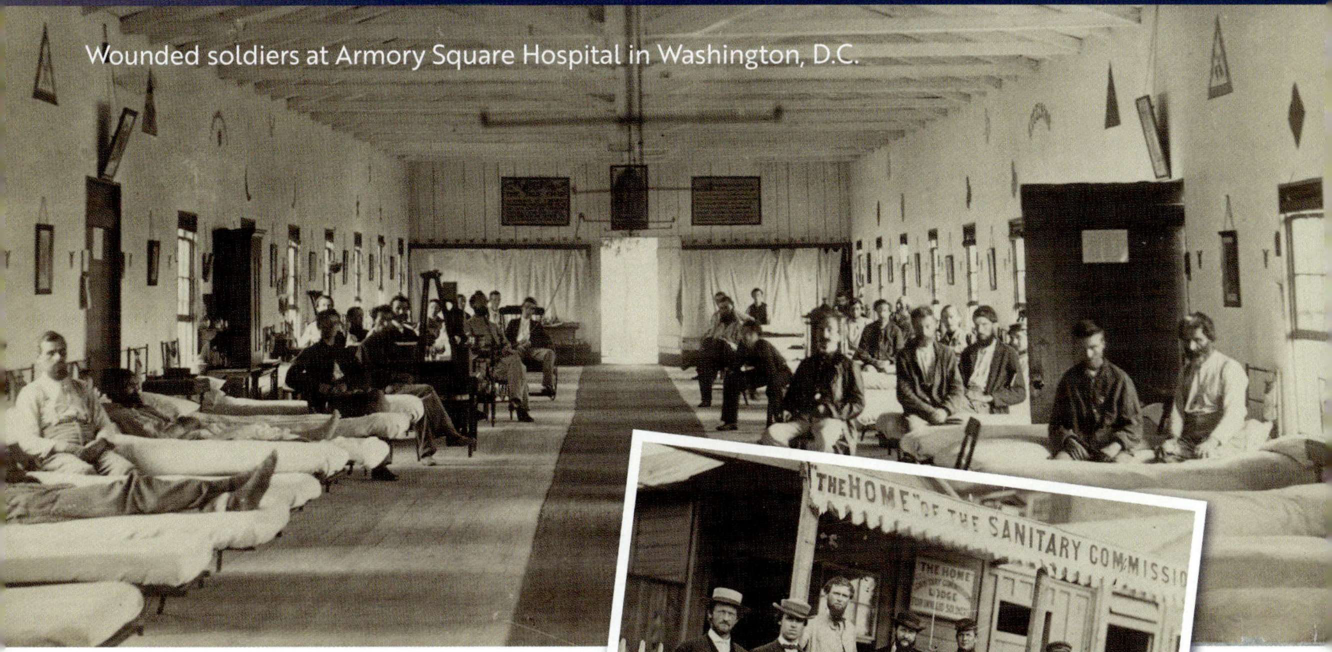

Wounded soldiers at Armory Square Hospital in Washington, D.C.

Sanitary Commission Lodge supporting sick and wounded soldiers

By the end of the war, many hospitals were well designed and clean. Doctors and nurses were better trained, and they kept records on their patients. Soldiers were sorted according to how severe their injuries were. The most severely injured were treated first. This system is still used today.

Dr. Elizabeth Blackwell
Feb. 3, 1821 – May 31, 1910

Dr. Elizabeth Blackwell was the first woman physician in the U.S. She helped establish the Sanitary Commission in 1861. Volunteers collected food, clothing, bandages, and medicine for Union troops. They cleaned and organized. They planned healthy meals for patients. The Commission advanced the efficiency and sanitation of hospitals.

CHAPTER FOUR

CULTURE AND COMMUNICATION

Information traveled quicker than ever during the Civil War. Messages could be sent long distances over telegraph lines. Lines were strung across the country and into army camps.

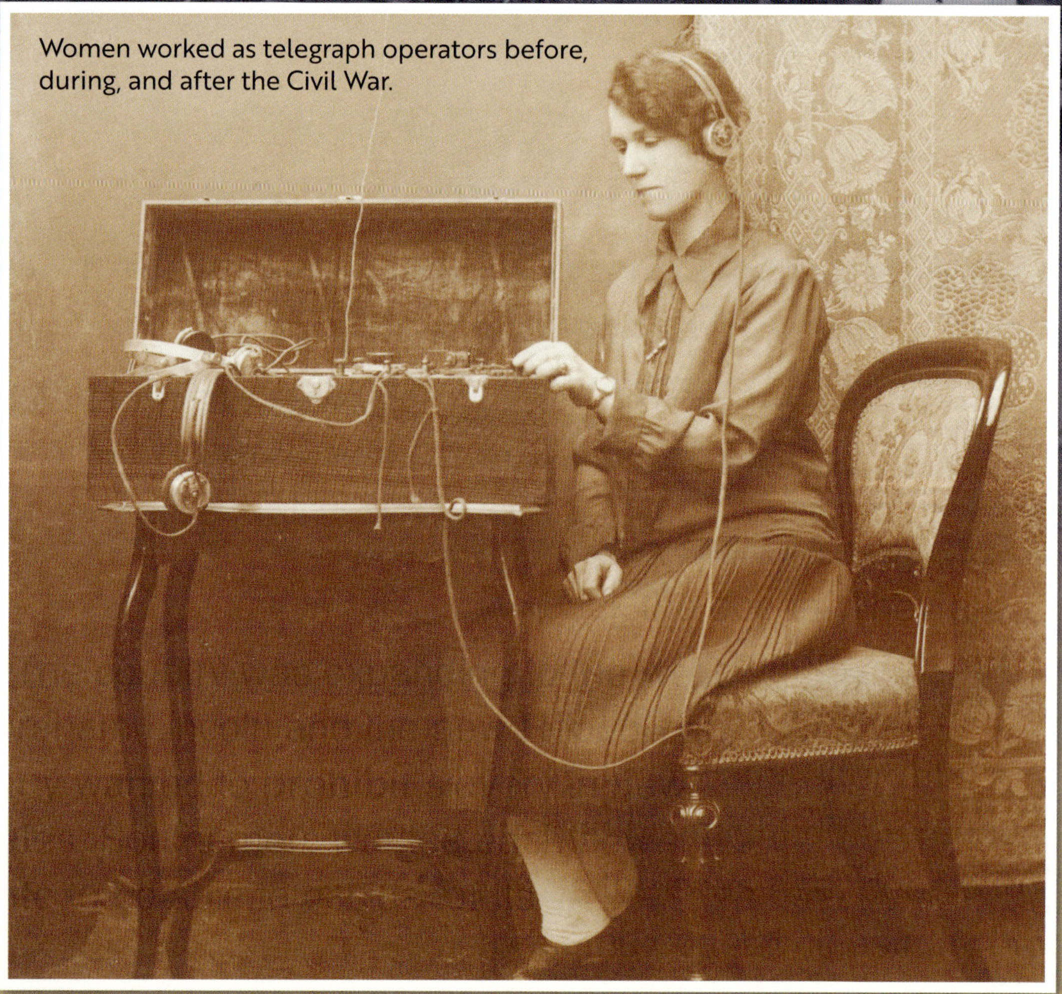

Women worked as telegraph operators before, during, and after the Civil War.

America had the most newspapers of any country. Reporters covered battles. Many soldiers wrote letters for their hometown papers. Artists sketched army life and combat. People at home could read about the war and scan the **casualty** lists for loved ones. Illustrated newspapers brought the terrible reality of the war into every home.

This poster was a recruitment tool used to bring in more soldiers for the Union army.

A vendor sells newspapers from a horse-drawn cart.

Mathew Brady was one of America's earliest photographers. He hired a staff of photographers to take pictures in army camps and on battlefields. In 1862, he exhibited the photographs at his studio in New York. Photos of injured and dead soldiers shocked Northerners and changed their view of the war.

Mathew Brady
May 18, 1822 – Jan 15, 1896

Music was one way civilians and soldiers distracted themselves from the horrors of war. Patriotic marches and sad ballads became popular.

Union forces sang songs such as "Yankee Doodle Dandy" and "The Star-Spangled Banner." "Dixie" and "When Johnny Comes Marching Home Again" were sung in the South.

Members of the 9th Veteran Reserve Corps pose with their instruments in April 1865.

Slaves created folk songs based on African music styles. These songs lifted their spirits and expressed their hopes for freedom. Slaves also sent secret messages about escape through song. Jazz music grew out of this African-inspired music. Jazz is the most influential music created in America.

CHAPTER FIVE

DAILY LIFE

The Civil War affected the lives of all Americans, northern and southern, free and slave. Most Americans supported the war effort in some way. Up to three million fought as soldiers, and others worked in army camps.

Men and women reenact the Battle of Big Bethel in Newport News, Virginia, which took place in 1861.

At home, men and women kept businesses and farms going. They raised money and gathered supplies for the armies.

Emancipation Proclamation

In the American Civil War, many times family fought against family, sometimes even brother against brother.

Africans remained enslaved in the South throughout the war. On January 1, 1863, President Lincoln signed the Emancipation Proclamation. It declared that all slaves in the states at war with the Union were free. Because the Confederate states considered themselves a separate nation, they ignored the proclamation.

A Confederate soldier's portrait illustrates how young many were who fought.

Most soldiers for both armies were **amateurs**. They were not well trained or well paid. They often lacked proper uniforms and supplies. They had little food to eat. Their lives were hard and dangerous.

Soldiers were supposed to be 18 or older, but boys as young as 10 or 12 served as drummers and even fought in both armies. Sometimes families followed soldiers to camps. Women and children helped with cooking, nursing, and other jobs. Some Southerners brought slaves to war with them.

The Emancipation Proclamation also made it legal for black men to join the U.S. army. Approximately 180,000 African Americans served in the U.S. Army. Among the first to sign up were Charles and Lewis Douglass. They were sons of Frederick Douglass, an escaped slave and famous abolitionist.

A soldier guards a fleet of Napoleon cannons.

Sojourner Truth, born Isabella Bomfree, was a slave in New York in 1797. She was forced to do hard physical labor, punished violently, and was bought and sold four times. In 1827 she ran away. An abolitionist family helped her sue for the return of her son, who was illegally sold in Alabama. Sojourner became a vocal advocate for abolition, civil rights, and women's rights. Because of her work, she was invited to meet President Lincoln in 1864.

Sojourner Truth
c. 1797   November 26, 1883

Many Northerners lived far from the action of the war. Their lives continued much the same as before. Adults went to work, and children went to school. But many families in the North had husbands, brothers, and sons away at war. At the same time, farms and businesses were growing to supply the war effort. Women and children filled many of the jobs vacated by the soldiers.

Black people, both wealthy and poor, lived in the North. Some owned their own businesses and were well educated. Most, however, had trouble finding good jobs. They were paid less than whites for the same work.

Cities offered public education for all children but had separate schools for white and black people. The schools for white children were much better than those for black children.

Students at a school for black children study corn and cotton.

Mary Jane Patterson
Sept 12, 1840 – Sept 24, 1894

Oberlin College was the first college in America to admit black students, beginning in 1835. Mary Jane Patterson, a former slave, graduated from Oberlin in 1862. She was the first African-American woman to earn a college degree. She became the principal of the first public high school for black students in Washington, D.C. in 1871.

People gather at the site of a home destroyed by Confederate forces on July 12, 1864.

Southerners suffered more during the war. They faced shortages in food, clothing, and medicine. People who lived near battles often had their homes and farms destroyed or taken over by soldiers. Thousands became homeless. Women struggled to feed their children.

Prices rose as goods became scarce in the South. Many families struggled to find food they could afford. In April 1863, several hundred women marched before the governor's mansion in Richmond, Virginia. They shouted, "Bread! Bread! Our children are starving while the rich roll in wealth."

Some slaves continued to work for their owners. More chose to flee north. As the Union army entered the South, many African men joined the troops. Their families often followed and lived in camps nearby.

Former slaves cross Union lines in a mule-drawn covered wagon.

CHAPTER SIX

CHANGING ROLES OF WOMEN

When men marched off to war, the women of the North and South got to work. In addition to their usual duties caring for homes and children, women took on more responsibilities. Southern women managed slaves. They picked cotton and harvested wheat and other crops. Southern women also helped defend their homes from Union soldiers.

In the North, women took over jobs vacated by men. They ran businesses and stores. They worked in offices. They made weapons, gunpowder bags, and other goods in factories.

Elizabeth Keckley (1818-1907), a former slave, opened her own dressmaking business in Washington, D.C. She became one of the most famous dressmakers in the North. She made fashionable dresses with wide skirts for wealthy women, including Mary Todd Lincoln, the President's wife. Mary and Elizabeth later became close friends.

Emily Blackwell
October 8, 1826 – September 7, 1910

During the American Civil War, Emily Blackwell helped organize the Women's Central Association of Relief, which selected and trained nurses for service in the war. Emily, her sister Elizabeth Blackwell, and Mary Livermore also played an important role in the development of the United States Sanitary Commission. Emily and Elizabeth helped women medical professionals gain acceptance in the U.S.

Women and girls on both sides volunteered any time they could spare. They made bandages and clothes for soldiers. They sewed flags. They raised money for much-needed food and supplies for soldiers.

This sketch depicts the fashionable dresses of the 1860s.

Women and children help with the cooking and cleaning for the 31st Pennsylvania Infantry.

Women could be found on the war front too. Some helped out in military camps cooking meals, mending clothes, and doing laundry. Others worked as nurses. They helped rescue and tend wounded soldiers. They often worked in dangerous conditions.

Hundreds of women fought as soldiers on both sides. They disguised themselves as men and joined the ranks. Most were not identified as women unless they were injured or killed.

Jennie Hodgers
Dec 25, 1843 - Oct 10, 1915

Jennie Hodgers served in the Union army for more than three years. As Private Albert Cashier, she marched thousands of miles and fought dozens of battles. She continued to live as a man after the war. She was buried with full military honors after her death in 1915.

Others risked their lives as spies. Women, and even girls, carried information and supplies across enemy lines. They hid messages within their wide skirts and parasols.

Miss Major Pauline Cushman
June 10, 1833 - Dec 2, 1893

Pauline Cushman was an American actress who worked as a spy for the Union army during the Civil War. At one point, she was caught spying on the Confederate army and nearly executed. After the war she traveled with P.T. Barnum and told stories of her exploits during the war.

Women worked hard and suffered many hardships during the war. But they also proved that they could work at jobs previously held only by men. They learned that they could take control of their lives.

Mary Walker
November 26, 1832 – February 21, 1919

Mary Walker served as a military doctor during the war. At first, army officials refused to consider her. She volunteered at tent hospitals, proving herself. In 1863, she was made an official army surgeon. She was the only woman to receive a Medal of Honor at the end of the war.

CHAPTER SEVEN

REUNITING THE NATION

The Grand Review of the Armies was a military procession and celebration.

On April 9, 1865, Confederate General Robert E. Lee surrendered his Army Union General Ulysses S. Grant. It was the beginning of the end of the war.

Families reunited. Former slaves were hopeful about the future. Then, just five days later, President Lincoln was shot and killed. The nation's recovery would not be easy for anyone. It would be another 16 months before President Andrew Johnson could declare the war officially over.

This painting depicts the assassination of President Lincoln in Ford's Theatre.

A black farmer harvesting corn

Black farm owners and brothers

The years after the war are called the Reconstruction Era. This time period, from 1865 to 1877, is also known as Reconstruction. This is when the government began to rebuild, or reconstruct, the South. Many of its cities and plantations had been devastated by the war.

During Reconstruction, many former slaves left the South. They wanted to escape the poverty and fear there. Thousands headed west to Kansas to make a new start. They built sod houses. They planted wheat on the fertile plains. Black people who migrated to the western plains became known as "Exodusters."

A family drives their wagon and mule team purchased with the help of the U.S. government's Farm Security Administration.

Amendments to the Constitution abolished slavery, gave former slaves citizenship, and extended voting rights to black men.

Black men were elected to office for the first time in American history during Reconstruction. Many won seats in Congress. Hundreds held offices across the South. They were important role models for the black community. They served despite insults and even violence.

This sketch shows white and black men placing their voting ballots into a ballot box.

The Freedmen's Bureau issuing rations to the old and sick

Congress established the Freedmen's Bureau. The Bureau provided newly freed slaves with food, medicine, and clothing. It set up schools and colleges for black students.

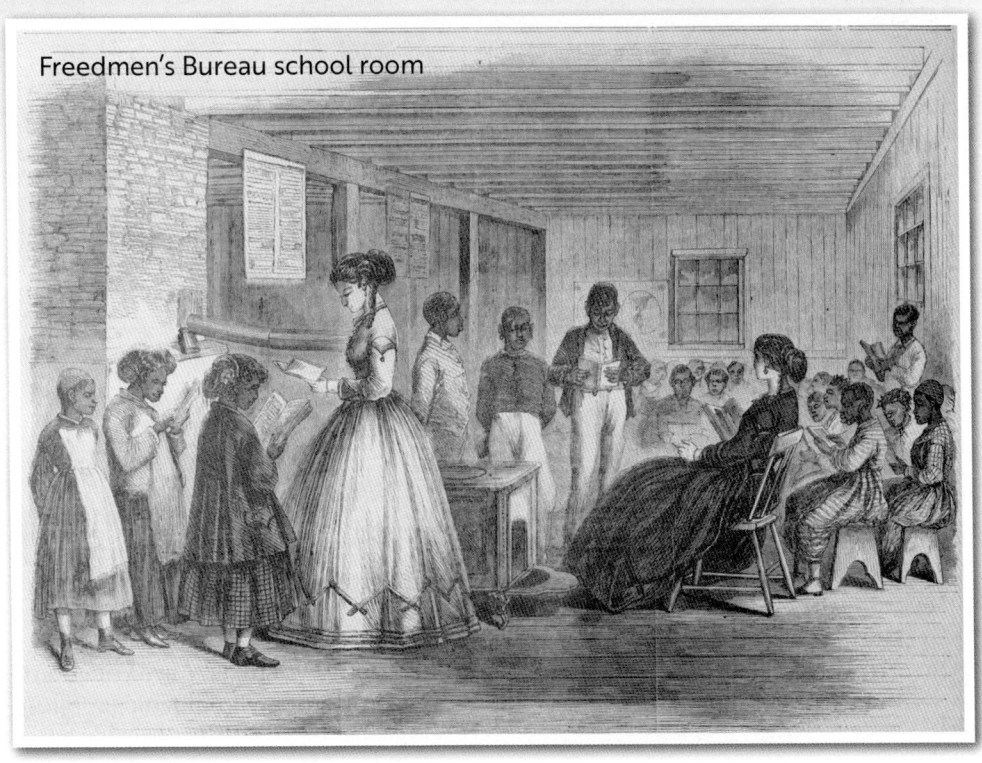
Freedmen's Bureau school room

Life was still difficult for former slaves. Few could get good jobs. Many returned to plantations as poorly paid workers. Laws were passed in the South that limited the freedom of black people. Other laws segregated, or separated, black people from white people. Segregation didn't end until 1964.

Mrs. Mary Crane, an 82-year-old ex-slave

Plantation living quarters

The Civil War determined the kind of country the U.S. would become. It established a strong central government. The Freedmen's Bureau was the first of many social welfare programs to help people in need. The women's rights and Civil Rights movements gained momentum. In many ways, the Civil War defined America.

Two veterans shaking hands

The Civil War preserved the Union and ended slavery, but America still had much work to do to ensure unity and equality for all people.

Gettysburg Celebration in Pennsylvania

GLOSSARY

abolish (uh-BOL-ish): end officially

amateurs (AM-uh-turs): people who lack skill or expertise to do a job

casualty (KAZH-oo-el-tee): a soldier listed as killed, injured, or missing at the end of a battle

Confederate (kon-FED-ur-et): a person or soldier from the states that seceded from the United States during the Civil War

currency (KUR-uhn-see): the form of money used in a country

plantations (plan-TAY-shuhns): large farms that need many workers

prohibit (PRO hi-bit): to forbid

sanitation (san-i-TAY-shuhn): clean and sanitary conditions

telegraph (TEL-i-graf): a device for sending messages over a distance

Union (YOON-yuhn): the states that remained in the United States during the Civil War

Index

abolitionist(s) 13, 29
Civil Rights movement 44
Confederacy 7, 8
Emancipation Proclamation 27, 29
Fort Sumter 8
Freedmen's Bureau 43
Lincoln, Abraham 6, 7, 8, 17, 27, 40
Reconstruction 41, 42
secede 7
segregation 44
slavery 5, 6, 10, 13, 15, 42, 45,
soldiers 9, 19, 20, 21, 23, 24, 26, 28, 29, 32, 34, 35, 37, 38
Stowe, Harriet Beecher 5
Tubman, Harriet 15
Underground Railroad 13, 15

Show What You Know

1. Why did the Civil War start?
2. Which states formed the Confederate States of America?
3. What was the Underground Railroad?
4. What work did women do during the Civil War?
5. Explain how the war affected daily life for people in the U.S.

Further Reading

Robertson, James, *The Civil War: 1861 – 1865,* Abbeville Kids, 2016.
DK Eyewitness Books, *Civil War,* DK Children, 2015.
Halls, Kelly M. *Life during the Civil War,* Core Library, 2015.

ABOUT THE AUTHOR

Yvette LaPierre lives in North Dakota with her family, two dogs, and two crested geckos. She works at the University of North Dakota and writes and edits books and articles for children and adults.

© 2019 Rourke Educational Media

All rights reserved. No part of this book may be reproduced or utilized in any form or by any means, electronic or mechanical including photocopying, recording, or by any information storage and retrieval system without permission in writing from the publisher.

www.rourkeeducationalmedia.com

Photo Credits: istock.com, Shutterstock.com. Library of Congress. Cover; Courtesy of the Library of Congress; Pg4/5; Library Of Congress, Hal Jespersen CCA-3.0, NoDeroq, Júlio Reis CCA-3.0, duncan1800. Pg6/7; Library Of Congress, Alexander Gardner (1821-1882). Pg8/9; Library of Congress. Pg10/11; Library Of Congress, Pg12/13; Studio-Annika, Library Of Congress. Pg14/15; Library Of Congress, BlackAperture. Pg16/17; Library Of Congress, Pg18/19; Library Of Congress, Winchester. Pg20/21; Library Of Congress. Pg22/23; cmannphoto, Mathew B. Brady, cjp. Pg24/25; Library of Congress. Pg26/27; FlamingPumpkin, CatLane. Pg28/29; Library Of Congress, Pg30/31; Library of congress, Oberlin College-WikiCCA-3.0. Pg32/33; Library Of Congress. Pg34/35; Library of Congress. Pg36/37; Library of Congress. Pg38/39; Library Of Congress. Pg40/41; Library of Congress. Pg42/43; Library of Congress. Pg44/45; Library of Congress

Edited by: Keli Sipperley

Produced by Blue Door Education for Rourke Educational Media. Cover and Interior design by: Jennifer Dydyk

Living Through the Civil War / Yvette LaPierre
(American Culture and Conflict)
  ISBN 978-1-64156-415-1 (hard cover)
  ISBN 978-1-64156-541-7 (soft cover)
  ISBN 978-1-64156-664-3 (e-Book)
Library of Congress Control Number: 2018930435

Rourke Educational Media

Printed in the United States of America, North Mankato, Minnesota